WHAT IS MAGNETISM?

LAURA LORIA

Britannica
Educational Publishing

IN ASSOCIATION WITH

ROSEN
EDUCATIONAL SERVICES

Published in 2015 by Britannica Educational Publishing (a trademark of Encyclopædia Britannica, Inc.) in association with The Rosen Publishing Group, Inc.
29 East 21st Street, New York, NY 10010

Distributed exclusively by Rosen Publishing.
To see additional Britannica Educational Publishing titles, go to rosenpublishing.com.

First Edition

Britannica Educational Publishing
J.E. Luebering: Director, Core Reference Group
Mary Rose McCudden: Editor, Britannica Student Encyclopedia

Rosen Publishing
Hope Lourie Killcoyne: Executive Editor
Nelson Sá: Art Director
Michael Moy: Designer
Cindy Reiman: Photography Manager
Amy Feinberg: Photo Researcher

Library of Congress Cataloging-in-Publication Data
Loria, Laura, author.
What is magnetism?/Laura Loria. — First edition.
    pages cm — (Let's find out! Physical science)
Audience: Grades 3-6.
Includes bibliographical references and index.
ISBN 978-1-62275-497-7 (library bound) — ISBN 978-1-62275-499-1 (pbk.) — ISBN 978-1-62275-500-4 (6-pack)
1. Magnetism—Juvenile literature. I. Title.
QC753.7.L67 2015
538—dc23
                                                                                              2013049194

Manufactured in the United States of America

Photo Credits
Cover, p. 1 (magnet) revers/Shutterstock.com; cover, p.1 (background), interior page borders Kompaniets Taras/Shutterstock.com; p. 4 Jeffrey Coolidge/Digital Vision/Getty Images; p. 5 Monty Rakusen/Cultura/Getty Images; p. 6 Roman Sigaev/iStock/Thinkstock; pp. 7, 28 © Robin Sachs/PhotoEdit; p. 8 Ivancovlad/Shutterstock.com; pp. 9, 14 Dave King/Dorling Kindersley/Getty Images; p. 10 Claire Cordier/Dorling Kindersley/Getty Images; p. 11 Peter Reid (peter.reid@ed.ac.uk); p. 12 Chicago Tribune/McClatchy-Tribune/Getty Images; p. 13 BananaStock/Thinkstock; p. 14 Dave King/Dorling Kindersley/Getty Images; p. 15 BlueRingMedia/Shutterstock.com; p. 16 Joel Arem/Photo Researchers/Getty Images; p. 17 Universal Images Group/Getty Images; p. 18 Pornchai Kittiwongsakul/AFP/Getty Images; p. 19 © The Photo Works/Alamy; p. 20 CBCK/Shutterstock.com; p. 21 Charles D. Winters/Photo Researchers/Getty Images; p. 22 Spencer Platt/Getty Images; p. 23 Liu Jin/AFP/Getty Images; p. 24 Bloomberg/Getty Images; p. 25 Design Pics/David Chapman/Getty Images; p. 26 © Lyroky/Alamy; p. 27 © Photodisc/Thinkstock; p. 29 © Cindy Charles/PhotoEdit.

CONTENTS

Magnetism

When you bring home an A-plus paper, where do you put it? On the refrigerator, of course! You grab a magnet and the paper stays up for everyone to see. But how does it stay up? The answer is magnetism.

Magnets can be used to hold items in place.

Magnetism is a natural force that can either bring certain metal objects together, like a magnet and a refrigerator door, or keep them apart. Some rocks and metals contain this power naturally.

Magnetism is an invisible force—it can be felt but not seen. Scientists study magnets, observing how they behave to understand how magnetism works.

THINK ABOUT IT

Magnetism is a force of nature, or something that happens without any known cause. Can you think of any other forces of nature?

Magnets can be simple objects used to hold items on a refrigerator or they can be parts of large, complicated machines.

Inside a Magnet

Everything in the world is made up of tiny units called **atoms**. Inside atoms are protons, neutrons, and electrons. When electrons spin around the center of the atom, tiny magnetic forces are created. If most or all of the electrons spin in the same direction, the magnetic forces join together to make a magnet.

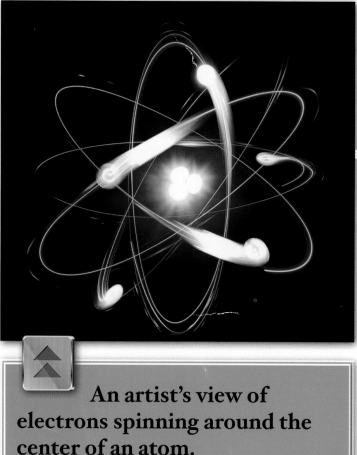

An artist's view of electrons spinning around the center of an atom.

Magnets can be made by rubbing a piece of metal in one direction against an existing magnet many times. The spinning electrons in the metal are pulled by the magnet in one direction, which creates magnetic force.

Atoms are what scientists call the units that make up all matter. The center of an atom is called a nucleus.

Running a needle over a bar magnet makes the needle magnetic itself.

Hard and Soft Magnets

Everything in nature has magnetism. Even objects such as wood or plastic contain some magnetism, but it is very weak.

Some magnets have electrons that move in one direction no matter what is happening around them. These are called hard, or permanent, magnets. It is difficult to change the magnetism of hard magnets. Other materials, such as iron, are soft, or temporary,

Horseshoe magnets are a type of hard, or permanent, magnet.

magnets. They are attracted to hard magnets but are not themselves permanent magnets. Some soft magnets can be made into hard magnets when heated, shaped, and cooled in the presence of a hard magnet.

Hot steel poured into molds can be cooled to form magnets.

POLARITY

Every magnet has two poles, or ends: a north pole and a south pole. If opposite poles are held near each other, they will come together. However, holding like poles near each other makes them repel, or push away from, one another.

Earth has two poles as well. Does this make the planet a magnet? The answer is yes! Earth is a large but weak magnet. Its magnetism is strongest near its geographic poles.

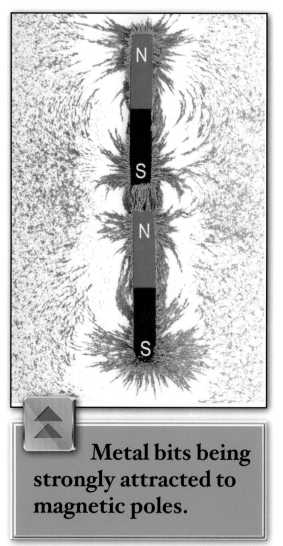

Metal bits being strongly attracted to magnetic poles.

What would happen if Earth's magnetism were stronger? What might happen to magnetic objects on or near our planet?

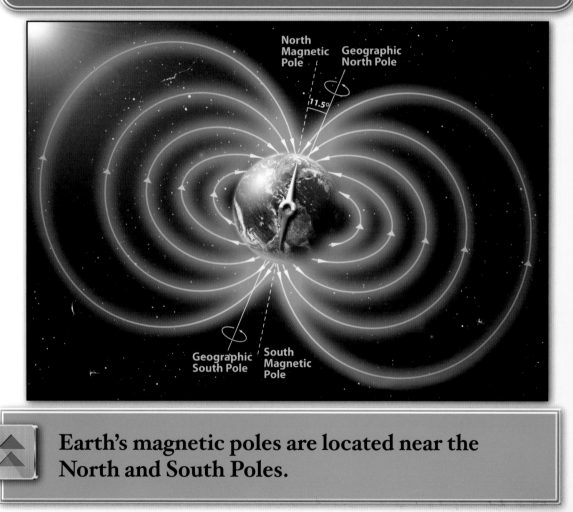

Earth's magnetic poles are located near the North and South Poles.

MAGNETIC FIELDS

Magnets do not need to touch objects in order to attract or repel them. Magnetic force works through air, water, and even nonmagnetic objects. For example, if you put a piece of paper between two magnets, they will still act as if nothing separated them. The area around a magnet that contains the magnetic force is called a magnetic field.

Magnetic force is often strong enough to operate despite physical barriers.

A compass uses Earth's magnetic field to show direction. One end of the magnet in a compass is attracted to the north magnetic pole. The magnet is mounted so that it is free to turn. That way the magnet always points north no matter what direction you are facing.

A compass gives directions using Earth's magnetic field.

THINK ABOUT IT

In what situations do you think a compass would be useful?

ELECTROMAGNETISM

Both magnetism and electricity are natural forces caused by the movement of electrons. An electric current flowing through wires creates magnetic fields. An electric current can be used to create magnetism, and magnetism can be used to create an electric current. They are partners in the creation of energy. Applying electricity to a wire

 Changing how wires are connected to battery terminals changes magnetic flow.

coiled around an iron rod creates an electromagnet. These are types of soft magnets that can be turned on and off by controlling the electric current. Electromagnets are used in all sorts of everyday things, from microwaves to doorbells.

COMPARE AND CONTRAST

Examine a battery. What does it have in common with a bar magnet? How is it different?

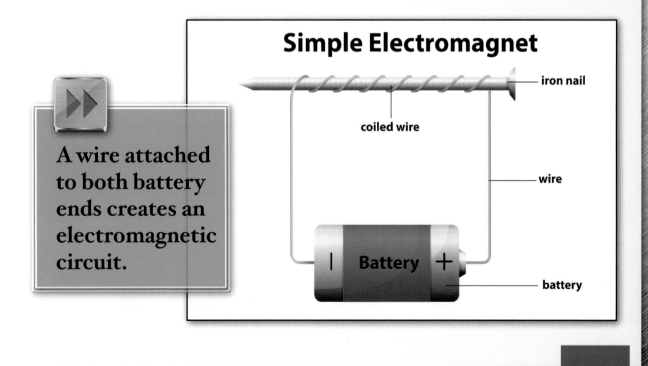

A wire attached to both battery ends creates an electromagnetic circuit.

Simple Electromagnet

iron nail

coiled wire

wire

Battery

battery

HISTORY OF MAGNETISM

Magnets were discovered, rather than invented. The first natural magnets, called **lodestones**, were discovered by the ancient Greeks and Chinese. After rubbing metal on these stones, the metal would itself become magnetic. Lodestones were used for religious and spiritual ceremonies for thousands of years. The Chinese began using them as compasses for navigation about one thousand years ago.

Many centuries passed before people began to understand why a compass

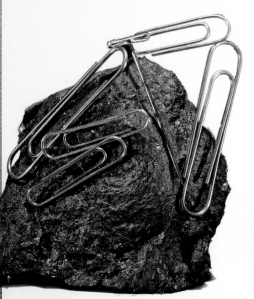

Magnetite, a natural lodestone, attracts paper clips.

A lodestone is a natural magnet.

needle always pointed north. William Gilbert, a doctor from England, was the first to prove that Earth itself is a giant magnet. In the 1800s, Hans Ørsted of Denmark observed the relationship between electricity and magnetism, leading to the discovery that electric currents can create a magnetic field.

Everyday Magnets

People use magnets every day in a variety of ways. Refrigerator doors have magnets in them to keep the doors closed and sealed. The headphones that you use to listen to music or to play games also have magnets in them.

Magnets are a part of electric motors used in many household tools and

Magnets help carry sound through headphones.

appliances. Even some toys, including a drawing board that uses metal filings, use magnets.

A magnet moves metal shavings around, allowing the user to "draw" using this toy.

THINK ABOUT IT

Many toys containing magnets have warnings printed on their labels about the danger of swallowing them. Why do you think it is dangerous to swallow magnets?

Magnets in Electronics

Any electronic device that creates sound, pictures, or motion uses magnets. Electromagnets are used in switches, such as those used for doorbells, that turn the current of electricity on and off. They are also present in home security systems. When two magnets are separated by opening a window or door, the magnetic force

Pressing a button closes the electromagnetic circuit of a doorbell.

is broken, causing the alarm to go off.

The hard drive in a computer stores information magnetically. Older televisions and computer monitors use magnets to spread electrons out into a picture. Smartphones could not vibrate without the use of an electromagnet.

A magnet held near an older "tube" video monitor shows the magnetic field inside.

COMPARE AND CONTRAST

Older "tube" televisions and video monitors use magnets to create images. Compare those to the newer LCD computer screens, which do not use magnets. Which would you rather have?

MAGNETS IN MOTION

Magnets create electricity in generators and motors. In newer hybrid and electric cars, hard magnets are used to create needed horsepower, while keeping the engine small and lightweight.

Modern roller coasters use magnets to create a thrilling ride. At the beginning of the ride, magnets repel each other for the initial push off. During the ride, magnets can slow down or speed up the cars, using attraction or repulsion. Even the

◄◄ Pulling a lever releases the magnetic force keeping this ride from moving forward.

Horsepower is a measure of mechanical power. One **horsepower** is strong enough to move 33,000 pounds (15,000 kilograms) a distance of 1 foot (30 centimeters) in one minute.

brakes used to stop the cars at the end of the ride are magnetic.

Maglev, or magnetic levitation, trains may be the long-distance transportation of the future. Instead of riding on a track, these trains use magnetism to hover over the track. Maglev trains are able to travel safely at speeds of 300 miles per hour (483 kilometers per hour).

A maglev train coming to a stop in China.

Magnets in Industry

On a construction site, magnets are very useful. Large electromagnets mounted on cranes attract heavy pieces of metal and lift them up. The crane then moves the metal to the place it needs to go. When the electromagnet is turned off, the metal piece is dropped in place. Magnets can also be used to pick up small pieces of metal, like nails, from the ground to prevent injury to the workers and damage to machines.

A worker controls a magnet to lift heavy steel coils in Australia.

In a factory, magnets might be used to hold screws or nails in place to be tightened by machines. On an assembly line, magnets can pick up and move into place metal parts that are used in making products.

Recycled metal is pulled off a pile by an industrial magnet.

Magnets in Medicine

Magnetic bracelets, sold as a pain-relief method.

Hundreds of years ago, doctors thought that magnets could pull diseases from the body and cure poisoning, baldness, and arthritis. Although some people believe that magnets can cure painful illnesses, scientists have not been able to prove it.

Magnets do have a very important use in medicine, though. Magnetic resonance imaging, or MRI, machines create a magnetic field around a person, which causes the body's protons to face in one direction. Energy that is released by the protons is captured by a magnetic coil in the machine. This is used by a computer to create a three-dimensional (3-D) image of the inside of a person's body on a monitor for a doctor to examine.

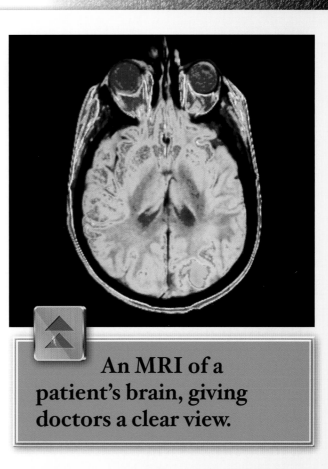

An MRI of a patient's brain, giving doctors a clear view.

COMPARE AND CONTRAST
MRIs give clearer pictures than X-ray images but are more expensive and take longer. If you were a doctor, which one would you use to examine a broken leg?

EXPERIMENTS TO TRY

Now that you have learned what magnetism is, you can experiment with magnets at home to see how they work.

Turn a Needle into a Magnet

For this experiment you will need a strong magnet and a sewing needle. Hold the needle by its eye. Take the magnet and brush it along the length of the needle in one direction approximately thirty times. Your needle is now magnetic. Test it by holding it near other metal objects, and see if you can feel the attraction.

A needle rubbed on a magnet creates magnetic force.

The Paper-Clip Challenge

This experiment requires a magnet, a paper clip (or a nail, as shown below), and a clear glass of water. Drop the paper clip into the glass of water. Using the magnet only on the outside of the glass, see if you can get the paper clip out of the water without getting your hands wet.

Magnets can move metal, even through glass.

GLOSSARY

assembly line A moving pathway in a factory where goods are put together piece by piece.

attract Pull toward; opposite of "repel."

compass A device that uses a magnet to tell direction.

current The flow of electricity.

electromagnet A piece of metal that is magnetized by an electrical current.

electrons Parts of an atom whose motion creates magnetism.

experiment A test of a scientific idea.

force A power of nature.

geographic Relating to the physical location of a thing.

hard magnets Objects that keep their magnetism.

hazardous Posing a danger to one's health or safety.

levitation The act of rising above the ground.

magnetic field An area in which there is a magnetic force.

magnetic resonance imaging (MRI) A medical technology that makes images of the inside of a person's body.

magnetism An invisible force that attracts objects to one another.

navigation The act, activity, or process of finding the way to get to a place when you are traveling in a ship, airplane, car, etc.

observed Watched carefully or noticed.

poles Two ends of a magnetized object.

repel Push away; opposite of attract.

soft magnets Objects that can be made magnetic but can lose their magnetism.

For More Information

Books

Eboch, Chris. *Magnets in the Real World*. Minneapolis, MN: ABDO Publishing, 2013.

Midthun, Joseph. *Magnetism*. Chicago, IL: World Book, 2012.

Schuh, Mari C. *Magnetism* (Blastoff! Readers). Minnetonka, MN: Bellweather Media, 2008.

Spilsbury, Richard. *What Is Electricity and Magnetism? Exploring Science with Hands-on Activities.* Berkeley Heights, NJ: Enslow Elementary, 2008.

Weakland, Mark. *Magnets Push, Magnets Pull.* Mankato, MN: Capstone Press, 2011.

Websites

Because of the changing nature of Internet links, Rosen Publishing has developed an online list of websites related to the subject of this book. This site is updated regularly. Please use this link to access the list:

http://www.rosenlinks.com/lfo/magn

INDEX